W9-AJL-538

Table of Contents

Rourke
Educational Media

A Division of
Carson Dellosa Education

rourkeeducationalmedia.com

Can you find these words?

candy

heart

love

married

We Celebrate Valentine's Day!

Valentine's Day comes in February.

3

Let's learn about Saint Valentine.

He helped people get **married** long ago.

Let's make valentines.

6

heart

Use a **heart**, glitter, and stickers.

7

Let's trade valentines!

Give one to each friend.

Let's give gifts.

candy

Give flowers and **candy**.

Let's say, "I **love** you!"

love

Give hugs and kisses too.

Did you find these words?

Give flowers and **candy**.

Use a **heart**, glitter, and stickers.

Let's say, "I **love** you!"

He helped people get **married** long ago.

Photo Glossary

 **candy** (KAN-dee): Sweet food made from sugar, syrup, chocolate, or nuts.

 **heart** (hart): A shape with a point at the bottom and two rounded parts at the top. Also an organ that pumps blood through the body.

 **love** (luv): A feeling of affection and warmth for another person.

 **married** (MAR-eed): Joined together with a partner.

Index

About the Author

Lisa Jackson is a writer from Columbus, Ohio. She likes to ride her bike and collect pennies. Her favorite holiday is the one that is coming up next!

www.rourkeeducationalmedia.com

PHOTO CREDITS: Cover: ©manonallard; Pg 2, 10, 14, 15 ©seb_ra; Pg 2, 13, 14, 15 ©kirin_photo; Pg 2, 6, 14, 15 ©RyanJLane; Pg 2, 8, 14, 15 ©By Sergey Novikov; Pg 3 ©Evgeny Sofrygin; Pg 4 ©By Zvonimir Atletic, ©wilpunt; Pg 12 ©kirin_photo

Edited by: Keli Sipperley
Cover and interior design by: Kathy Walsh

Library of Congress PCN Data
Valentine's Day / Lisa Jackson
(Holidays Around the World)
ISBN 978-1-73160-576-4 (hard cover)(alk. paper)
ISBN 978-1-73160-451-4 (soft cover)
ISBN 978-1-73160-625-9 (e-Book)
ISBN 978-1-73160-688-4 (ePub)
Library of Congress Control Number: 2018967333

Printed in the United States of America,
North Mankato, Minnesota